P9-CNH-270

GABRIELLE DOUGLAS
Raising the Bar

ZONDERVAN®

ZONDERVAN.com/
AUTHORTRACKER
follow your favorite authors

ZONDERVAN

Raising the Bar
Copyright © 2013 by Gabrielle Douglas

This title is also available as a Zondervan ebook.

Visit www.zondervan.com/ebooks.

Requests for information should be addressed to:

Zondervan, 5300 Patterson Ave. SE, Grand Rapids, Michigan 49530

Library of Congress Cataloging-in-Publication Data

Douglas, Gabrielle, 1995–
    Raising the bar / Gabrielle Douglas
      pages   cm
    ISBN 978-0-310-74070-4 (hard cover : alk. paper)
    1. Douglas, Gabrielle, 1995- 2. Women gymnasts—United States—
Biography. 3. Women Olympic athletes—United States—Biography. I. Title.
GV460.2.D68A3 2013
796.44092—dc23
  [B]   2013004067

Cover design: Cindy Davis
Cover photography: Keith Cephus
Interior design: Alexea Rhodes, Bokmeow Media
Feature pages written by Michelle Burford

Printed in Mexico

13 14 15 16 17 18 19 20 /DRM/ 20 19 18 17 16 15 14 13 12 11 10 9 8 7 6 5 4 3 2 1

Table of Contents

Regular Teen,
AMERICA'S CHAMPION

Gabrielle Douglas is

THE FIRST AFRICAN AMERICAN AND FIRST WOMAN OF COLOR FROM ANY NATION
TO WIN A GOLD MEDAL IN THE INDIVIDUAL GYMNASTICS ALL-AROUND COMPETITION

THE FOURTH AMERICAN FEMALE GYMNAST
TO WIN THE GOLD

THE FIRST U.S. GYMNAST
TO RECEIVE BOTH OF THOSE HONORS IN A SINGLE OLYMPIC GAMES

Those are big accomplishments for a four-foot eleven-inch sixteen-year-old from Virginia. But she is still a normal American teen who is figuring out who she is and what's next in her life. Dive into Gabrielle's world from her perspective, and get to know this bubbly athlete who stole America's heart and made an entire country cheer.

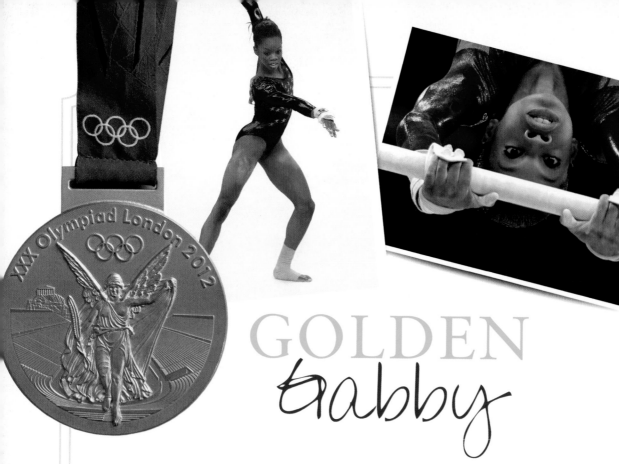

GOLDEN
Gabby

Birthdate:
DECEMBER 31, 1995

Birth Order:
YOUNGEST OF FOUR

Siblings:
ARIELLE, JOYELLE, JOHNATHAN

Birthplace:
NEWPORT NEWS, VIRGINIA

Parents:
NATALIE HAWKINS
AND TIMOTHY DOUGLAS

Furry Family Members:
ZOWAY AND CHANDLER

Current Residence:
WEST DES MOINES, IOWA

School:
HOME SCHOOL AND
ONLINE TUTORING

Sport:
WOMEN'S ARTISTIC GYMNASTICS,
STARTED AT SIX YEARS OLD

Club:
CHOW'S GYMNASTICS AND DANCE
INSTITUTE

Connections

MY FAMILY AND FRIENDS

The Real Superstars: My Fam

My gymnastics dreams have only been possible because I have one thing: the love and support of my amazing family. Laughing and relaxing with them away from the gym made all those training hours easier to get through. Of course, I have to give so much credit to my mother: Do you have any idea how many sacrifices she made to pay for my training? She worked long hours just so she could have the money to take care of our family, as well as invest in my dream.

The rest of my family also sacrificed too: My sister Arielle gave up ballroom dancing and Joyelle stopped ice-skating so Mom could afford to keep me in my sport. They've done everything possible to support me. And when I was hundreds of miles away in Iowa, they cheered me on from Virginia. Joy and I often Skyped or called each other after watching our favorite TV shows. I talked to Mom almost every day, and Arielle and John usually got on the line afterward. What a gift my family has been to me!

In a way, I've been blessed twice: I was born into the best family a girl could ask for (really!), and I then found a second family in Iowa. When Travis and Missy Parton took me in, their love and encouragement made the hard days a little less difficult. If you have to be away from your mom, sisters, and brother, I've gotta tell you, the Parton home is a great spot to land. Travis, Missy, and the girls became an extended family for me. I will always be grateful for my two families—they're all-around golden.

My Family

I laugh a lot with my family. We all tell hilarious stories, and we like to climb into my mom's bed and hang out there. My mom has been with me through thick and thin, the tough and the rough.

Mom
NATALIE HAWKINS:

"There's no greater joy than for a parent to see their child reach their dream."

Natalie Hawkins
@livlonglivstrng

My kids have me over here laughing hard! Love it when we are all together—it's a straight comedy show!

Sister
ARIELLE:

"I taught her a cartwheel, then the next day I saw her doing one-handed cartwheels and I thought, *I didn't teach you that, that's not part of the lesson until a week from now.*"

Arielle Hawkins
@ArieHawk

Love hanging with the fam @gabrielledoug @livlonglivstrng @DJoybells & @dougieFfresh25! We seriously need our own show #NeverADullMoment lol

Sister
JOYELLE:

"I was so happy when my sister was on the podium. I just kept thinking, *She did it—she won!*"

Joyelle Douglas
@DJoybells

Congrats to my beautiful sister @gabrielledoug for being awarded Sports Women of the year! You look absolutely fantastic ;)

Johnathan Douglas
@dougieFfresh25

My sis @gabrielledoug was the first African American to win gold in 2012 At London Olympic games … We DID IT @ gabrielledoug YOU DID IT sooooo proud of you

Gabrielle Douglas
@gabrielledoug

@dougie128 You have always been there for me when times got tough every minute you were right there supporting me and telling me to NEVER give up no matter what! I couldn't have asked for a better brother. I love you SO much words can't even describe!

Brother
JOHNATHAN:
Johnathan and Gabrielle are best friends.

Grandfather
THEODORE HAWKINS:
Oprah nicknamed Gabrielle's grandfather Theodore "Mr. Subtle" when she interviewed him after the Olympics. He likes wearing his Gabby T-shirt, the one that says "Flying Squirrel" on the front and "Gabby's Grandpa" on the back.

USA

Kellogg's
CORN
FLAKES
The Original & Best

SINCE 1906

GABBY DOUGLAS

I AM SO GRATEFUL GOD HAS TRULY BLESSED ME. REMEMBER TO ALWAYS GIVE HIM THE GLORY FOR HE IS GREAT!

Right at Home

I moved to Iowa when I was fourteen to train at a new gym with a new coach. It was a big sacrifice. I never would've guessed that I'd wind up with another awesome family out of it. Meet my family away from home: Travis, Missy, Hailey, Lexi, Leah, and Elissa Parton. Travis feels like a big brother and a father to me.

"WITH FOUR GIRLS ALREADY, ADDING ANOTHER ONE WAS PRETTY EASY. AS LONG AS SHE'S IN MY HOUSE, SHE'LL BE TREATED AS ONE OF MY DAUGHTERS."
—TRAVIS PARTON

"The Partons provided such an amazing home for her, and she needed that father figure. And I'm so blessed that she has that in Travis."
—Mom, Natalie Hawkins

"We've created a family. It's not your typical family. Family goes beyond genetics and beyond the color of your skin. She is just like one of the family, so it doesn't feel like she is 'extra'!"
–Missy Parton

My Big Brother

My mother, who sacrificed so much for me to become a gymnast, will always be at the top of my list of heroes. My brother, John, is a close second. He's only fourteen months older than me, yet John has always been so protective: Way back when we were toddlers, John once saw another little boy push me out of a toy car; John pushed that boy out of the car and pulled me back in. And let the record show that even when my sisters and I persuaded Mom to let me move to West Des Moines, John wasn't so thrilled at first. "If you send her to Iowa," he said, "how will I be able to protect her all the way from Virginia?!"

John still supported me—to the point of giving me a pep talk when I later wanted to give up on my dream. "You've got to make a living in your sport," he told me one night on the phone from Virginia Beach. "Today should always be better than yesterday. You've got to put your body on the line. Remember our motto: If you want to be the best, you've got to take out the best." Suddenly that evening, the lights came on: I had to stick with my goal if I ever wanted to make it to London. Less than seven months later, I was standing on top of an Olympic podium, feeling such gratitude for the family member I admire so much for his strength, courage, and wisdom—my big brother.

Inspired by Champions

DOMINIQUE DAWES: Dominique competed in three Olympic Games! And she was the first African American woman to win a gold medal in artistic gymnastics. How could I not be inspired by her? Even though I was too young to see her first two Olympics live, after watching her performances, I wanted bigger and better skills. After I won gold, Dominique interviewed me. It was amazing!

TIM TEBOW: NFL star Tim Tebow inspired me to speak out about my faith. I don't think I could have done it if he hadn't been so bold about his own faith during interviews and on TV.

CARLY PATTERSON: In 2004, I set my sights on the Olympics—all because of Carly Patterson. I'd been practicing giants (a fully extended 360-degree swing) on the uneven bars. I was so excited to see Carly do the exact same move on TV. Then she won the gold. Goose bumps! That's when I chose to work harder so I could stand on the same podium one day.

London 2012

London 2012

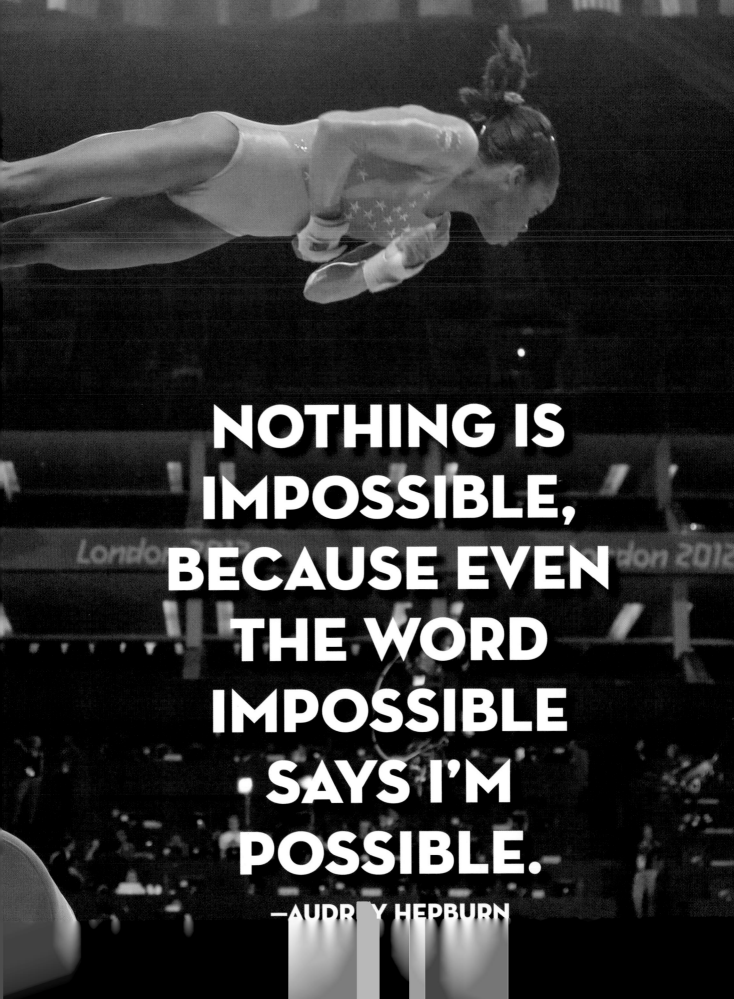

NOTHING IS
IMPOSSIBLE,
BECAUSE EVEN
THE WORD
IMPOSSIBLE
SAYS I'M
POSSIBLE.

—AUDREY HEPBURN

Blessed With BFFs

I still have my friends from back when I started gymnastics. But I don't get to see them a lot when I'm traveling and training, which means we keep in touch on Twitter.

My first best friend was Kaiya Putnam. We met at Gymstrada in Virginia Beach. I called her my giggling buddy. We trained and did school work together at the gym. When Kaiya stopped training at Excalibur, my new gym bestie was Beka Conrad. We had sleepovers, created our own obstacle courses, worked on homework at the library, and roller skated. I missed her when I moved to Iowa.

Beka Conrad
@B_Convicttt

On my way to va beach to finally see Gabby!!

It was sad to leave my friends in Virginia to move to Iowa. But I found new friends at Chow's gym and on my Olympic team. I've been blessed with so many good friends each time my life changes.

Gabrielle Douglas

@gabrielledoug

Practicing the freakum dress dance by beyonce with @Aly_Raisman before our flight. Slow and steady improvements ;) @nekaijo would be proud

Aly Raisman

@Aly_Raisman

@gabrielledoug you are the first person I've ever had a dance party at the airport with... Loving it.

On the Olympic tour with Kellogg's, I still got to spend lots of time with my teammates and other Olympians. I love sushi dates with my friend Anna Li and going for pho (a Vietnamese dish) together.

When training for the Olympics, everyone on the women's gymnastics team spent a lot of time together. We didn't get to skip out to go hang with our families. A lot of the time, we sat on the couches, stuck our feet in ice buckets (good for soothing sore joints and muscles!), and watched the show *Awkward*.

Me and my old teammate Britany Ranzy

My Fierce Five Teammates

JORDYN WIEBER

KYLA ROSS

MCKAYLA MARONEY

ALEXANDRA RAISMAN

My Higher Power

My mother raised me and my siblings with a rock-solid faith in God. She wanted us to know that no matter what happened in our lives, God would always be there to strengthen us and care for us. For a while when I was around nine, my family observed some of the Jewish traditions. My mother has always felt a strong connection to Judaism, and so did my grandmother. That's why our family went to Shabbat services at a Jewish synagogue in Norfolk, Virginia. We also celebrated Hanukkah during the holiday season. One year, Mom bought us each a dreidel, a four-sided spinning top, which we played with while the song "Twinkle, Twinkle Candle Bright" filled our house. At first, my brother and sisters and I were cool about switching from Christmas to Hanukkah—until we realized we wouldn't decorate a tree.

Eventually, Mom had to work on the weekends so she could earn the money for us to get another car (ours broke down!), and we stopped attending the synagogue. But even then, Mom wanted us to really understand what we believed and continue studying it. "I'm not going to choose a path for you," she'd often tell us, "but I want you to always explore the truth. God gives us all free will to choose what we will believe."

I did eventually make my own choice: I am a Christian. When I won those two gold medals in London, I knew the whole world was watching me.

My Life
INSIDE MY WORLD

#chillin!

Relaxing . . . what's that? Since the Olympics, I've hardly had a moment to sit down. What a whirlwind! I've done everything from perform in the Kellogg's Tour of Gymnastics Champions (phew!) and appear on the cover of *Essence* magazine (it's strange to walk through airports and spot my picture), to starring in a Nintendo commercial and throwing out a pitch for a New York Mets baseball game.

As much fun as all that is, I realize how important it is for me to just chill. Want to hear something shocking? Because my life is so full and busy, relaxing is about doing . . . absolutely . . . nothing.

I have the best time when I'm sitting around in my PJs, surfing through TV channels and catching up on a few shows, or simply joking around with Arielle, Joy, or John. When I'm on the road, sometimes Arielle and Mom come along with me (love that!). Our version of painting the town red is hanging out in our hotel room, ordering room service, and talking about both the old times and the new experiences we're having. That's hardly boring when we've been in nonstop motion for weeks.

Whenever I get the chance, I return to my hometown, Virginia Beach. I love walking along the shore, catching up with friends, and eating at some of the restaurants that my family and I enjoyed when I was much younger. Yet even when I go home, it's a different reality: People recognize me! One time when I was trying to disguise myself with a hat and sunglasses, some guy still knew it was me. "Hey—there's that gymnast!" he said. I guess I need a better disguise, LOL!

Inner Tubes and Pixy Stix

When I get me time, I want to go to the beach or lounge on my bed. Hanging out in my room is when I like to text, tweet, listen to music, and upload photos to Instagram.

Gabrielle Douglas
@gabrielledoug

Ahhh feels good to back on the beach!! Soo glad I got to visit the beach!! Chillen!!

IN IOWA: I like to go swimming with Missy and her four daughters at the pool or float on inner tubes. In the winter, we'd also go sledding. (I wasn't supposed to sled before the Olympics so I wouldn't get hurt, but I did go on a small hill! People waited at the bottom to catch me if I wiped out.)

BACK HOME IN VIRGINIA BEACH: My favorite place to go with my brother and sisters is to Jody's Gourmet Popcorn shop. They have all kinds of flavored popcorn, fudge, pixy stix, and candy. It's like a Willy Wonka store. For big fun, we head to King's Dominion, Busch Gardens, Motor World, or Water Country USA.

WHERE I'D CHOOSE TO GO ON VACATION: Hawaii

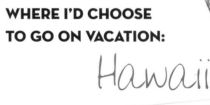

A Girl's Gotta Eat

Being a gymnast uses so much energy, so I love to eat.
Some of my favorite foods . . .

Snacks:

GOLDFISH CRACKERS
MINI PRETZEL STICKS AND HUMMUS
FRUIT

Fast food:

MCDONALD'S

Dessert:

WARM APPLE PIE WITH VANILLA BEAN ICE CREAM ON TOP,
CHOCOLATE-COVERED STRAWBERRIES

So good!

Breakfast:

STRAWBERRY-STUFFED FRENCH TOAST
WITH WHIPPED CREAM

Home-cooked meal:

MOM'S MATZO BALL SOUP AND MISSY'S HAM BALLS
(MADE OF HAM, SAUSAGE, AND BEEF, MIXED WITH GRAHAM
CRACKER CRUMBS, THEN GLAZED WITH A MIXTURE OF TOMATO
SOUP, BROWN SUGAR, DRY MUSTARD AND VINEGAR)

Types of food:

MEXICAN OR ITALIAN

Ice cream:

COOKIES 'N' CREAM

I REFUSE TO GIVE UP. I REFUSE TO QUIT. I PUSH TOWARD MY DREAM, KNOWING THAT IT WILL BE MY REALITY.

London 2012

Stuff I Like

I listen to music all the time, even during competitions! When I have some time to myself, I like to read, knit, or watch TV.

My choice of music:
UPBEAT, ESPECIALLY HIP-HOP AND COUNTRY

My favorite artists:
TAYLOR SWIFT, KATY PERRY, EFFERVESCENCE, AND BEYONCÉ

My favorite books:
TWILIGHT SERIES

My favorite TV show:
THE VAMPIRE DIARIES

My sister Joyelle and I liked watching a lot of the same shows growing up, such as *Bratz*, *Wildfire*, and *H2O: Just Add Water*.

Taylor Swift
@taylorswift13:

@GabrielleDoug, just read in People how you said you listen to my songs when you warm up—that made my day!!

Gabrielle Douglas
@gabrielledoug

Wow The Vampire Diaries gets better and better every episode!! Love love it!!

S. DAKOTA MINNESOTA

WISCONSIN

MICHIG.

IOWA

ILLINOIS

INDIANA

Midwest Fun

When I'm not training or doing school work in Iowa, I love having fun with my host family, the Partons. I have a bedroom upstairs near the girls, and the whole family eats dinner together. Nobody misses dinnertime at the Partons'. The girls and I like playing in the backyard on the trampoline. I help Leah with her gymnastics skills out there—but we love just jumping around!

For fun, Gabrielle and I go to lunch at Panera, watch the show *Dance Moms*, and chat.
—Missy Parton

FOR FUN, GABRIELLE AND I GO TO MOVIES, WALK AROUND THE LAKE, AND HAVE "DATE NIGHTS." —TRAVIS PARTON

Sunday is our down day. We get up and go to church together, grab some lunch, and then spend the rest of the day just relaxing at home. We might watch TV, nap, play outside if it is nice, but mostly enjoy time together with no schedule!
—Missy Parton

#grounded

I grew up going to church in Virginia Beach. Even when my family didn't attend a Sunday service, Mom would still gather us around for Bible study. One of my favorite stories is about Daniel and the lion's den, which Mom would read to us from the Amplified Bible. After Daniel, a hard worker and a prayer warrior, was placed in a powerful position during Babylonian times, others around him began plotting to get rid of him. So they convinced the king to pass a law that would make praying a huge no-no—and if someone was caught praying, the person would be sent to the lion's den. Whoa.

Daniel never stopped praying, which is why he was thrown into that den full of lions. Not even facing one of the scariest situations imaginable was enough to make Daniel get off his knees! That took some serious courage. Just the thought of walking into a den of hungry lions makes me feel jittery. But you know what? God protected him. The lions didn't touch Daniel.

Whenever I'm feeling afraid, I remember Daniel's bravery. I also think about the dozens of Bible stories and Scripture my mother passed on to me —like the one I will always love: "I can do all things through Christ, who strengthens me" (Philippians 4:13 NKJV). Before every gymnastics meet, I ask my heavenly Father to give me his strength. Never once has he let me down. Even during those competitions when I make a mistake or get nervous, I know God can see something that I can't—the big picture. He knows what he needs to teach me and where he needs to take me. I have to trust him to carry me there—just like Daniel did.

I GIVE ALL GLORY TO GOD. THE GLORY GOES UP TO HIM, AND THE BLESSINGS FALL DOWN ON ME.

Before the Olympics, my host mom, Missy, asked my friends and family to write letters. She dated each one so I could read one a day during the Olympics. I am so thankful for all the wonderful words people sent with me.

The excerpt below is from my mom's letter, which I read on July 11, 2012, the day I left for Olympic Preparation Camp.

Gabrielle,

. . . Listen, as you prepare today to go out there and WOW the crowds, remember one thing. Have fun and enjoy yourself! Rebuke nervous energy and allow your inner fierceness to take over. It is time to SHINE BRIGHT, my love. Take in every single moment. Remember, you were created for such a time as this . . .

As you think back to the day that I put you in gymnastics (I remember that day like it was yesterday), I felt a feeling of such pride when the gym's owner came out to ask me how much gymnastics experience you had gotten because he recognized your talent from the first time he saw you. And over the years, as everyone would exclaim to me how amazing you were, I was filled with such gratitude that God would deem me worthy to entrust such a precious gem to me . . .

I hope that as you realize your dream, you will always remember God's faithfulness. Remembering His goodness has been what has seen me through many difficult and joyful times. He has truly blessed you, my love. Go out and SHINE for His Glory . . .

I believe this is your time. Seize your moment without hesitation. It is yours—now walk in it!

All my love,

Ma

Hey Breezy!

I just want to start by saying that I am sooooo proud of you! You are just so strong and have been so dedicated to this sport, to your dream. It's kind of funny that even though you're my li'l sis, I look up to you for inspiration and motivation to do what I need to do in my own life. You have worked so hard to get to this point and have sacrificed so much for your dream. Don't let anything or anyone stand in the way of you making your full dream come true!

I know that this time in London will probably be the hardest, most tiring, and most difficult time in your life. But in the end, after all of your hard work, it will prove to give you some of the best and most memorable moments that you will have to cherish and hold on to forever . . . Remember that God and His Angels are always with you and will help you whenever you are in need . . .

I was just so happy to see you finally reach the top at the Olympic trials, but that was only the beginning of what you can do with the strength and talent that God has given you. You're soooo close to making your full dream come true. It's just right there waiting for you to reach out and grab . . .

LOVE YOU!!!!

Arie

#beingme

Knowing who you are—that's a pretty important part of growing up. When you get to know yourself, you start to like all the little things that God created you to be. What makes me unique? There are hundreds of small things as well as big ones. For instance, I love to wear bright colors like yellow, red, green, and blue. I think they look great on my skin tone. I also love flowers. I always sniff them. Love the smell! It's so amazing to me that they can come in so many shapes, colors, and sizes.

And have I mentioned that I was once really interested in country music? Now, I'm more into upbeat music by singers like Beyoncé, Pink, Miley Cyrus, Katy Perry, and Taylor Swift. So part of getting to being you is about knowing what you like and what your tastes are—and I like so many things!

What else make me, me? My principles—the things I believe in and stand for. In my case, it's things like honesty, kindness, integrity, forgiveness, hard work. Others know who I am not just by what I say, but by what I do. Every day, my goal is for my beliefs and actions to line up. Of course, we all make mistakes. There are days when I fall off track. That's why I'm so grateful to serve a God who knows my heart. He knows my intention is to do the right thing. Even when I mess up, he is always waiting to forgive me. Talk about grace!

Four-Legged Friends

I'm a sucker for cute animals—especially dogs. What could be more adorable than a furry puppy, staring up at you with big, beautiful, sweet eyes? It's enough to make my heart sing. I want to protect them as much as I want to curl up with them. I love them all—puppies, kittens, rabbits, you name it. What's not to love?

Even when I was a little girl, I wanted to rescue stray dogs around our neighborhood; my older sisters wouldn't hear of it. "No, Brie," Arielle and Joyelle would say. "What if he has rabies?" I begged Mom to get us a dog. She wouldn't—probably because she didn't need another thing to take care of! But one year after my friend Kaiya got the cutest little pooch, I gave Mom my own version of puppy dog eyes. "Please, Mom," I pleaded, staring up at her. "Not now," was always her answer.

One day after gym when Mom surprised me with a black, furry stuffed animal (her idea of a substitute!), I wasn't happy. Can you believe that when we got to the car, something bounced up when I opened the door? A black puppy! I practically leapt into my mother's arms as I bounded up and down. "Thanks, Mom!"

The pup was an eight-week-old black Labrador and Rottweiler mix that Mom got from a local Society for the Prevention of Cruelty to Animals (SPCA). We named him Zoway. Mom later gave us a second shock: Zoway got a little brother we call Chandler, a Maltese and Yorkie mix. Make that Chan Chan for short. And make that one very happy girl.

Big Lessons

FINDING MY STRIDE

Putting on My Big-Girl Pants

When I was fourteen, I took a big chance: I moved from my home in Virginia Beach to West Des Moines, Iowa. Why on earth would I go from a city near the beach to a freezing spot in the Midwest? Because I wanted to train with one of the best gymnastics coach's in the world, Liang Chow—and his training center is located in West Des Moines. That began one of the longest journeys of my life.

Isn't it funny how when you want something so badly—and then you finally get it—you often wonder why you wanted it in the first place? Don't get me wrong: I was warmly welcomed by the most loving host family I could've ever asked for. But I missed my own family. Terribly!

I daydreamed about what it would be like to just chill with Arie, Joy, and John on a Sunday afternoon. I missed my mother's home cooking. I missed the friends I'd left behind. In fact, I was so homesick at one point, I told Mom I wanted to quit and move back to Virginia Beach. "I know you miss home, Brie," she said, "but you've signed a contract that says you will represent your country to the best of your ability. You've got a responsibility to your teammates . . . If gymnastics is not your passion, then at the very least, you will finish the season . . ."

I knew Mom was right—but I still wanted to go home. And can I tell you how glad I am that Mom wouldn't let me? Every time I look at those two gold medals, a word pops into my head—perseverance. Without it, nothing great can be accomplished; with it, most dreams are within reach.

WHEN GABBY FIRST MOVED IN, I LET HER DECIDE THINGS SUCH AS WHERE SHE
WANTED TO SLEEP, GAVE HER CONTROL OF THE BATHROOM, MADE SURE THAT HER
BEDROOM WAS HER SPACE. IT TOOK HER A MONTH OR SO TO SPEAK UP WHEN SHE
NEEDED SOMETHING AND TO JOIN IN ON HER OWN.   —MISSY PARTON

Far from Home

Living with Travis and Missy Parton eased the heartache of missing my family. But I cried when I went to bed. I didn't know where things were in their house. At first, I couldn't bring myself to ask for things I needed. I'd call my mom to tell her I needed lotion or snacks. Then she would call Travis and Missy for me.

Now I can see how God set up the whole situation. Missy and Travis are such a blessing in my life. Training with Coach Chow would never have been possible if I didn't live with them. When I wanted to quit and go home, Travis and I had a tough conversation—a couple hours long! But he helped me stick it out.

[OUR CONVERSATION ABOUT QUITTING] WAS A DEEP MOMENT. I SAID, "WHATEVER YOUR CHOICE IS FROM HERE, WE'LL SUPPORT YOU, BUT THE DOOR ONLY GOES ONE WAY." IT WAS VERY TOUGH TO SAY, BUT I HAD TO LET HER KNOW THE REPERCUSSIONS.
—TRAVIS PARTON

I remembered the words Mom had left me with at the airport—her reassurance that no matter where I was, God was right there with me and that she was only a plane ride away.

FAITH IS BEING SURE OF WHAT WE HOPE FOR. IT IS BEING CERTAIN OF WHAT WE DO NOT SEE.

—HEBREWS 11:1 (NIrV)

Brain Training

I've always enjoyed school. Seriously. For pre-K and Kindergarten, Mom enrolled me in Greenhill Farms Christian Academy, a top private school in Norfolk, Virginia; my other siblings also attended there for a time. Mom says that even when I was very little, I could spell big words like *loquacious*. Sometimes I wonder how, at that age, I could even pronounce it, much less spell it!

Anyway, I loved learning new things and still do. I caught on to ideas quickly (just like in gymnastics!). During first and second grades, I attended Holland Elementary in Virginia Beach—and then from third grade on, I was homeschooled. Why? Because homeschooling makes it easier for a competitive gymnast to fit in all those hours of training.

In home school, I follow various online curriculums. During my first year, I followed the same curriculum used at Greenhill Farms Academy; later, Mom got me started with online courses. Tutors—and Mom, of course—guide me through the content and help me figure out any material that stumps me.

As much as I love reading history (Dr. King's "I have a dream" speech still gives me chills!), I have my other favorites like science and literature. When I was still enrolled in elementary school, there was P.E.—such a cake walk for someone who spends dozens of hours working out as a gymnast! Mr. Dule, my P.E. teacher, cheered me on as I cranked out pull-ups and worked my way up the hanging rope. If you're reading this, Mr. Dule, I have to say thank you. Long before the Olympics, you made me feel like a real superstar.

School Days

Back in Virginia Beach, I would go to school from 8:00 a.m. until 3:00 p.m. like most kids. Then I started home-schooling. (Shout out to all you homeschoolers!)

At my former gym in Virginia, my school hours were from noon to 2:00 p.m. In Iowa, I start schoolwork around 9:30 in the morning. Missy is home then too. At 2:15 p.m., Missy takes me to the gym for practice.

Who helps me with my schoolwork:
ONLINE TEACHERS
MY MOM

My favorite subject:
SCIENCE

I like experiments; it's fun to watch things bubble up. And I feel smart when I put on safety goggles.

Goal:
EARNING MY
HIGH SCHOOL DIPLOMA

THIS PAGE: TOP: RUSLAN DASHINSKY/ISTOCKPHOTO.COM; BOTTOM: PHOTODISC. FACING PAGE © LESLIE JEAN-BART

Homeschooling
Tools:

**BOOKS, EMAIL, VIDEO CHAT,
ONLINE TUTORING**

HOLY BIBLE

I PRAY THAT GOD WILL KEEP ME HUMBLE AND GROUNDED. I WANT TO BE A ROLE MODEL AND BE A BLESSING AND GIVE BACK TO THE PEOPLE WHO HAVE SUPPORTED ME.

#blessed

Every time I travel to camp or an international assignment, I have my Bible with me. I bring the big version in my suitcase and a small one in my purse. I highlight verses that my mom, family, friends, and fans send to me. I read them over and over to build up my faith.

One of my mom's favorite verses is Deuteronomy 28:13: "The LORD will make you the head, not the tail. If you pay attention to the commands of the LORD your God that I give you this day and carefully follow them, you will always be at the top, never at the bottom."

She kept reminding me of this verse during the months leading up to the Olympics.

One of my favorite Bible stories is Daniel and the Lions' Den. Daniel wasn't afraid to stand his ground—even when he was thrown down to face hungry lions. He knew he had God on his side. I love to read about him when I need to be bold, strong, and courageous.

"God didn't leave or fail Daniel, and He will never leave or fail you," Mom told us.

Icing my legs after training or competition prevents swelling and inflammation.

Gym Days

IN TEN YEARS OF GYMNASTICS, I'VE HAD ABOUT 18,000 HOURS OF TRAINING.

Here's a typical four- to six-hour day at the gym: A whole-body workout that includes thirty minutes of conditioning, followed by practicing sequences on vault, bars, beam, and floor. We end with about twenty minutes of conditioning and flexibility exercises.

When I'm learning a new move on bars, Coach Chow puts me in a secured belt and harness to learn the timing. Once he thinks I'm ready, we move to a pit full of squishy foam so when I land, I don't hurt myself. After that, it's time to practice the real thing—no extra help.

Days and Hours

Leading up to the Olympics, Coach Chow, his wife, Li, and I pushed it to the limit in the gym every day. And he added interruptions because I've had to learn how to block out distractions. Other gymnasts gather around the apparatus I'm on and shout and cheer and scream. That's important mental training!

CHOW'S GYM:

28
HOURS A WEEK

6
DAYS A WEEK
A MINIMUM OF

15
ROUTINES A DAY

AS I GET CLOSER TO COMPETITION, CHOW INCREASES THE DIFFICULTY LEVEL IN MY ROUTINES.

CHOW NEVER CLOSES THE GYM. WE DON'T GET SNOW DAYS.

It's All About the Kip

Have you ever tried something so many times that you just wanted to give up? For me, that was the kip—a really difficult gymnastics skill that I had to learn when I was eight years old. The kip is a common move that gymnasts perform on the uneven bars. To master it, you have to have great timing, strength, and momentum. The kip begins with pulling yourself up to the low bar in a swing glide, bringing your toes to the bar, hoisting your hips up, and finally holding your upper body above the bar. I worked on the skill for a year and couldn't make it happen. Sigh.

One Friday night, Mom took me to open gym so that I could work on my kip. Some of the girls in a higher level spotted me struggling and rushed over. "Need some help?" one girl asked. I did. By the end of the evening, the other gymnasts hadn't just helped me nail the kip; they'd given me a gift—a reminder that when you work hard enough at something for long enough, you can eventually master it. P.S.: I had a reminder of my success every time I looked down at my hand: the hugest blister had formed on my palm and then ripped open. As much as my hand hurt, it also made me feel proud.

As it turns out, learning the kip was the perfect preparation for all the tough skills that came after that. Like a round-off double back on the beam. Or a double pike dismount off the uneven bars. Or an Arabian double front leap combo on the floor. It's all pretty scary stuff, and each time I became frightened, I remembered what it felt like to finally pull of the kip. If the kip is possible, anything is possible. That's as true now as it was when I was eight.

A Positive Spin

Favorite Events

All along, I've loved to perform my floor routine and on the balance beam. I used to hate the uneven bars. I'd often tell Mom, "I'm never going to be any good at them." But Coach Chow changed how I felt, and my mom encouraged me to think positively about them. "A great bar routine is like a beautiful song—it should have nice rhythm and flow," Coach Chow told me. Team USA Coach Márta Károlyi's nickname for me (Flying Squirrel) came when she saw my performance on the uneven bars.

Favorite Move
PIKE TO TKATCHEV ON BARS

Uneven Bars

"Often a crowd favorite, the uneven bars demand excellent upper-body strength, split-second timing, and an aggressive approach. . . . The most daring parts of the routine are often in the high-flying release moves and dismounts. This event . . . requires courage and precision to be able to release and re-grasp the bars."

—USA GYMNASTICS

Balance Beam

4 FEET TALL—Just 11 inches shorter than I am

4 INCHES WIDE—Barely enough for a small foot

16.5 FEET LONG—Slightly longer than three of me lying down end to end

"The balance beam challenges gymnasts because they must execute routines that give the impression that they are performing on the floor. The beam routine may not exceed ninety seconds and must cover the entire length of the beam."

—USA GYMNASTICS

79

Floor Exercise

40-BY-40-FOOT SPRING FLOOR
COVERED IN FOAM AND CARPET

"The floor exercise gives gymnasts the chance to express their personalities through their music choice and choreography. Gymnasts often get energy from the crowd, and they usually welcome audience participation in clapping to the beat."

—USA GYMNASTICS

Vault

RUNWAY LENGTH: 78-82 FEET

VAULT HEIGHT: APPROXIMATELY 4 FEET

"Gymnasts perform complicated vaults in different body positions, such as tucked, piked, or stretched. The best vaulters are explosive off the springboard, as well as when pushing off the table. Speed, power, and spatial awareness are essential to performing high-level vaults correctly."

—USA GYMNASTICS

Terms

ALL-AROUND:

A category of gymnastics that includes all four of the events. The all-around champion of an event earns the highest total score from all events combined.

APPARATUS:

One of the various pieces of equipment

GIANT:

A swing in which the body is fully extended and moving through a 360-degree rotation around the bar

KIP:

Movement from a position below the equipment to a position above

"STICK" LANDING:

Slang term used for when a gymnast executes a landing with correct technique and no movement of the feet

TNT
Taught 'N' Trained

Where would I be without all the coaches I've had? They supported, encouraged, and pushed me when I needed it. I especially have to thank my coaches Liang and Li Chow and Márta Károlyi for helping me realize my dream of making the Olympic team.

My current coach, Liang Chow, motivates me by giving me goals each day. Coach Chow believed I could be an Olympic medalist when I first showed up in Iowa. What a huge vote of confidence! His personality has rubbed off on me too. I was a shy little girl when I got to Iowa, but Coach Chow was fun and bubbly. Now, we love to joke with each other and laugh.

THE JOURNEY OF TRAINING EVERY DAY— THE HARD WORK, THE EFFORT, THE IMPROVEMENT, THE PROGRESS— THAT'S MORE IMPORTANT THAN GETTING THE GOLD. THE VICTORY ISN'T JUST ABOUT EARNING A MEDAL; IT'S ABOUT WINNING EVERY SINGLE DAY THAT YOU TRAIN.

—COACH CHOW

THIS PAGE: JOHN W. MCDONOUGH/SPORTS ILLUSTRATED; GETTY IMAGES: FACING PAGE: TOP: PETER READ MILLER/SPORTS ILLUSTRATED/GETTY IMAGES. BOTTOM LEFT: STREETER LECKA/GETTY IMAGES: BOTTOM RIGHT: RONALD MARTINEZ/GETTY IMAGES

HARD DAYS ARE BEST BECAUSE THAT'S WHERE CHAMPIONS ARE MADE.

Rise to the Top

The more competitions you win, the more your confidence grows. One major boost to my confidence came in March 2012 during the AT&T American Cup at New York's Madison Square Garden. Jordyn Wieber and Alexandra Raisman had already been chosen to represent the United States at the meet, but Coach Chow still managed to get me into the competition as an alternate, where I could compete in exhibition routines and have my performance evaluated by the same judges who scored the official competitions. In the end, Jordyn claimed the title as all-round champion, an honor she deserved. Both she and Aly gave amazing performances.

Though my scores didn't count, I still ended up with the highest score at the event—and everyone took notice. In fact, many saw the 2012 American Cup as my coming out party. You know what? So did I. For the first time, I had proven to the world—and to myself—that I had what it took to compete with the best gymnasts.

After that, the media's coverage of me seemed to shift. The press began suggesting that I may be a real competitor at the London Olympics. Rather than relaxing after that huge confidence boost, I trained harder than I'd ever trained in my life. I knew that making the Olympic team was within my reach. I had to believe in myself, rely on God's strength, and follow my coach's guidance. The rest, as they say, is history.

Risky Moves

To get to the next best place in life, you have to have the courage to make a bold move. I learned that the year I was fourteen. I wasn't advancing in gymnastics at the rate I knew I needed to. I had a dream of going to the Olympics. But how would I get there if my skills weren't tough enough?

"If I'm going to make it to the Olympics, I need Coach Chow," I told my mother. "I want to move to Iowa and train with Liang Chow." As you can imagine, my mother thought this was a crazy idea. What mother would want to send her daughter to another state for nearly two years? Certainly not mine. "Have you looked at a map lately?" Mom said. "Iowa is nowhere *close* to Virginia Beach! There's no way I'm sending my baby across the country."

But I was convinced: I knew I had to train with a coach who believed in me—and could take me to the next level. After lobbying my mother for weeks (along with my sisters), Mom gave in because she also knew I needed to make that change. And I learned something else: When you really believe in something, you should push to make it happen. Then when it does happen, step confidently toward your new life. It might be a little difficult at first (nobody told me Iowa would be so cooooold!), but in the end, it might also be totally worth it. I have no doubt that my choice to move and train with Coach Chow led to my Olympic gold medals. But before I could get there, I had to stand up for what I knew in my heart.

Coming Back from a Crash

WHEN I GOT MY FIRST HUGE BLISTER FROM PRACTICING BARS SO MUCH, MY COACH TOLD ME, "GETTING A RIP IS A SIGN THAT YOU'RE A REAL GYMNAST." THAT LESSON OF ENDURING PAIN TO GROW AND IMPROVE CERTAINLY WASN'T THE LAST.

I had my first big injury—a fracture of the growth plate of my wrist—in 2009. Then in the summer of 2011, one year before the Olympic trials, I got hurt. I heard a pop in my leg while I was doing a leap while training at Chow's gym. I injured my hip flexor and hamstring. Not good timing since the National Championships were in August. As you can imagine, gymnastics is risky. Twists, trips, and falls are all part of training. I've been blessed that I've only faced a few physical obstacles:

- Countless bruises
- Continual blisters
- Busted lips
- Aching muscles that felt like I just fell down the stairs
- Stress fracture in my wrist
- Sprained hamstring
- Injured hip flexor—Yow!
- Severely sprained ankle
- Strained back
- Sore knees
- Lots of cuts

Physical therapy, cortisone shots, ice buckets, and ace bandages help me recover so I don't make an injury worse. But it's no fun to rest for weeks or compete with an injury.

90

My Sparkle
MORE THAN BLING

Protein, Veggies, and a Side of Twix

Let me get one thing straight from the start: I do like sweets. I used to be obsessed with M&M's, but now my favorite candies are Twix and Starbursts. A lot of people ask me whether a gymnast has a strict diet, and the answer may surprise you. Liang Chow, my coach, never told me what I should eat, but he did stress healthy eating habits. I've never had a problem with my weight; I've always had a small figure and a fast metabolism. Of course, I do still watch my diet. In other words, I don't eat junk all the time. I include a lot of protein (milk, chicken, eggs) to help my muscles recover after all of those difficult workouts. I also eat veggies and fruit to make sure that I'm getting plenty of vitamins. So even when I eat sugary foods, it's just a little treat here and there—not all of the time, or even most of the time.

When most of us think of health and nutrition, we usually think of food. But good health is also about rest. Plenty of it. Even though my schedule is very busy now, I do my best to get in at least seven or eight hours of zzzz's. This is especially important when I'm training—my body can only take so much hard work before I have to give it the chance to rest. And of course, I sip plenty of water throughout the day. Gotta replenish after all that sweating!

© JOHN CHENG (TOP 2)

Road Trippin'

Competitions, tours, and media appearances keep me really busy. With the Kellogg's Tour of Gymnastics Champions, we had rehearsals for eleven days, then toured forty cities. In between shows, I sometimes rode in the tour bus to the next city.

The bus had bunk beds, two living areas, a little kitchen, and a bathroom. It was cramped, but we made it cozy. Usually we were on the bus only at night. It was like a traveling hotel.

So we slept and snacked—lots of snacks. Sometimes we ate dinner on the bus. We had so much fun on the tour, because we were out there to entertain and give the audience a good show.

My coach and me with Shawn Johnson, Aly Raisman, Mckayla Maroney, Jordyn Weiber, and Derek Hough while on the Kellogg's tour.

Snackin' and Nappin'

TOP TO BOTTOM © PAUL JOHNSON/ISTOCKPHOTO.COM; MORTON OLSEN/ISTOCKPHOTO.COM; JILL CHEN/ISTOCKPHOTO.COM; EYEWAVE/ ISTOCKPHOTO.COM CAMILLA WISBAUR/ISTOCKPHOTO.COM; PAUL DRINKWATER/NBC/NBCU PHOTOBANK VIA GETTY IMAGES.

Since gymnastics events last only a few seconds or minutes in competition, gymnasts don't load up on food. I don't eat a lot during the day. For breakfast, I love to eat cereal or oatmeal. For lunch, I have maybe a sandwich and yogurt. After practice, I recharge and eat the most—dinner and lots of snacks until I go to bed.

BREAKFAST

LUNCH

DINNER

SNACKS!

I LIKE TO SLEEP—
MY BODY NEEDS IT!
I USUALLY SLEEP
EIGHT TO TEN
HOURS A NIGHT. ON
DAYS WHEN I HAVE
TWO PRACTICES, I
MAY EVEN TAKE AN
HOUR NAP IN
BETWEEN.

The perfect Leo (Leotard)

I had eight leotards just for the Olympics. As national team members, we don't have to pay for our leos. The price of leos can run up to $500. Would you believe that engineering is just as important as style? The wear test and the wash test determine if the leotard is ready for competition. No gymnast wants anything slipping out of place as she's flipping and leaping. Sometimes a leotard gets as much of a workout as I do! LOL

For some meets, I get to help design my leos. The sportswear company sends fabric swatches to me. Then my mom, host mom Missy, and my sisters help me choose the colors and designs. We get to see the initial concepts or create our sketches, and tell the designer what we like. At the first fitting, we see the leotards on a body for the first time.

THIS PAGE ON BOTTOM: EMMANUEL DUNAND/AFP/GETTY IMAGES. FACING PAGE: CHRISTIAN PETERSEN/GETTY IMAGES (LARGE). AL TIELEMANS/SPORTS ILLUSTRATED/GETTY IMAGES (SMALL)

I usually paint my nails to match my leo—purple, blue, orange, neon green, red . . .

INSPIRED BY THE CHRYSLER BUILDING IN NEW YORK CITY, the Olympic leotard had an elegant, art deco style. All the bling on it is Swarovski crystals (the real deal!).

ELASTIC AT
THE LEGS AND
NECK KEEP THE
LEO IN PLACE

EVERY LEO
NEEDS SOME
SPARKLE!

STRETCHY
COMPRESSION
FABRIC CALLED
MYSTIQUE HAS
SOME SHEEN
TO IT

LONG SLEEVES
LOOK MORE
DRESSED UP FOR
COMPETITION

My favorite leotard
from the Olympics
was the red one with
the Swarovski crystals.
Love those sparkles!

99

#girliegirl

I used to be a tomboy. My big brother, John, and I were practically joined at the hip as kids (we're just fourteen months apart!) so I wanted to copy him with everything, including how I dressed. That means that I, like John, wore a lot of sweatpants when I was around seven or eight. And my hair? It was usually back in a ponytail!

Fast-forward to age twelve—the year changed from a tomboy to a girlie girl.

My older sister Joyelle had a lot to do with that: She was always picking out the cutest clothes, and one time, I liked her outfit so much that I decided to begin experimenting with more feminine and fashionable choices. By the time I left for Iowa, I was kind of a fashionista. Mom and I shopped for jeggings (a cross between jeans and leggings), cute boots, and my first pair of heels.

"You need to go out looking good, or don't go out at all!" Mom would often joke with me. She was right: being stylish is one way to express yourself to the world, to let your personality shine through. My mom and I choose my clothes and accessories by how they look on me and how I feel when I wear them. But sometimes, I love to rock a label.

As for makeup, I prefer the natural look during competition. For special occasions, I enjoy dressing up and getting my makeup done, like for the Video Music Awards in 2012. So fun!

ALL THAT *glitters*

Yellow is
so happy
and bright.

I love
sparkles!

Love to wear
on the red carpet:
AN ABOVE-KNEE DRESS THAT SPARKLES

Favorite color:
YELLOW

Love to wear
in competition:
**LONG-SLEEVE VELVET LEOTARD
WITH RHINESTONES**

Love anything sparkly:
**PHONE, SHOES,
EARRINGS AND BRACELETS,
ON MY JEANS**

Gabrielle Douglas
@gabrielledoug

A special thank you to my Gold Medal Celebrity Hair Stylist! @tedgibsonbeauty

For gymnastics, like most athletes, I put my hair up in a half loop and clip down shorter pieces. I use Pantene balm for flyaways. Outside of the gym and competitions, I like to wear my hair down. But I love to have my hair done by a celebrity stylist, like Ted Gibson or even my Virginia hairstylist, Lakisha Bell.

Favorite place to shop:
LOS ANGELES

Favorite stores:
NEIMAN MARCUS, NORDSTROM, BCBG, LOUIS VUITTON, TOPSHOP (LONDON)

Favorite brands:
NIKE, MISS ME JEANS

Daily makeup:
FOUNDATION, MASCARA, EYELINER, BLUSH, LIP GLOSS

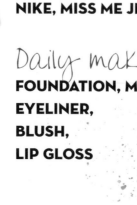

THIS PAGE TOP TO BOTTOM: MISSY PARTON; GABRIELLE DOUGLAS; CHRIS RATCLIFFE/BLOOMBERG VIA GETTY IMAGES; AP IMAGES/JENNIFER GRAYLOCK; KEDROV/SHUTTERSTOCK. FACING PAGE © KEITH CEPHUS

USE YOUR SMILE TO CHANGE THE WORLD; DON'T LET THE WORLD CHANGE YOUR SMILE.

Fun FACTS

CELEBRITY CRUSH:
Ian Somerhalder

I CAN'T LIVE WITHOUT
chocolate

THINGS I ALWAYS SAY:
"Really?!" and "Why thank you!"

IF I COULD HAVE A SUPERPOWER:
I'd be invisible

IF I COULD GO PRO IN ANY OTHER SPORT:
I'd take on Usain Bolt
in track! LOL

FAVE FOOTBALL TEAM:
New England Patriots

FAVE BASKETBALL TEAM:
LA Lakers

True Beauty

My mother taught me to appreciate my beauty—both inside and out. In our world, we pay so much attention to what we look like and what we wear that we sometimes forget to value what really matters—how we treat others and ourselves.

Of course, I still enjoy making the time to get cute! My mom is my stylist, but I also love picking out great outfits, shoes, and earrings. I haven't always been 100 percent confident in my beauty. I once went through a difficult time after an incident that really shook how I saw myself. I overheard one of my coaches say, "Yeah, she needs a nose job." I was shocked and hurt. I didn't tell Mom about it until much later, but I did start asking her questions.

"Mom, am I pretty?"

"Of course, Brie," she said. "You've always been beautiful."

"Was I cute even as a baby?" I continued.

"Yes," she replied. "Why are you asking me this?"

Mom knew something was bothering me. When I did finally reveal what I'd overheard, Mom was as hurt and upset as I was.

That experience taught me a big lesson: No one can make you feel inferior unless you allow them to. Thankfully, I am surrounded by a family who loves me and affirms me. The comment stung and I had to fight to prevent it from sticking. Why? Because I know that I am created in the image of a Father who cares so much for me—and how can anything created in God's image need a do-over? He also blessed me with a gymnastics gift that I can use to bring glory to him—that's what real beauty is all about.

My Journey

WHERE I'VE LANDED

Leaps and Bounds

My family didn't have a lot of money and wound up homeless for a short time after I was born. Not the beginning you would expect for an Olympic gymnast, is it? But gymnastics was in my blood. When I was a toddler, our apartment became my obstacle course. I dove off furniture, tumbled across the living room, jumped on the kitchen table, and even climbed to the top of a closet door. Can you tell that I didn't sit still much?

My sister Arielle taught me cartwheels when I was three then showed me spider-walk handstands, splits, bridges, and back walk-overs. Because my sister broke her wrist in two places while doing back handsprings, my mom wasn't interested in putting me in the sport. But at Arielle's urging (four years of urging, to be exact), my mom enrolled me in gymnastics when I was six years old. My first coach couldn't believe the raw talent he saw when I took my first trial class.

I never would have made it to the Olympics on my natural talent alone. From my sisters persuading my mom to let me move to Iowa to Coach Chow's training, it all led to two gold medals. It's amazing to look back on the path of my life and gymnastics career so far. I'm amazed at where I've landed. Thank you, God.

Gabrielle Douglas
@gabrielledoug

@Aly_Raisman Leotards=$300 Grips=$150 Realizing you're going to London as an Olympian....PriceLess

ALL THE
HARD WORK,
ALL THE
SACRIFICE,
OH MY GOSH,
SHE DID IT!
—NATALIE
HAWKINS

Passport to a New Point of View

Gymnastics has taken me all over the world (take a look at the map on the next page). The 2011 World Championships in Tokyo, Japan, was one of my most memorable trips abroad. When I arrived in Tokyo—my first time there!—the place was stunning. All over the city, I spotted green gardens filled with colorful pagodas. Wide and super-clean boulevards downtown. There were more bike parking lots than car parking lots. I also noticed another interesting thing. So many people ride bicycles in Tokyo.

Of course, my ultimate overseas adventure came in Summer 2012: my teammates and I traveled to London. It was an amazing trip! On our drive from the airport to the hotel, I caught a glimpse of the London Eye, that enormous Ferris wheel high above the city's skyline. When the wheel was first built back in 1999, it was the tallest one in the world.

I couldn't wait to ride on the London Eye. My teammates and I rode in one capsule, and my family rode in the capsule behind us. I was in awe as I looked out over the city with the Thames River winding through it. It was breathtaking!

For me, traveling is like reading—it's a kind of passport that immediately transports you from one reality to another. It's a way to peek into a new world, one with a seemingly endless horizon.

That's why, whenever I visit a new place, I always come home with a new point of view—and, sometimes, a medal. Fingers crossed that Rio, Brazil—home of the 2016 Olympics—will bring me the same. But regardless of what happens in the arena, I can be sure of one thing: I'll return with some amazing memories from a place known for its gorgeous beaches and sunshine. I can't wait!

On the Move

ST. PAUL, MINNESOTA
Big time discouragement hit me at the Visa National Championships in 2011. Competing with two injuries was no fun at all. This was the toughest competition of my career!

WEST DES MOINES, IOWA
Blood, sweat, and tears here to get to the Olympics. But this is also where my second "family," my host family, lives.

SAN JOSE, CALIFORNIA
The last big stop before the Olympics: the Olympic trials. My win guaranteed my spot on the US Olympic team.

GARY, INDIANA
Sometimes for the holidays, my mom takes us back to her hometown to visit both her mom's and dad's relatives. We have a really big family.

TULSA, OKLAHOMA
My family lived here for the first few months of my life.

RICHARDSON, TEXAS
Childhood home where I loved to crawl over everything and dive off our furniture.

IRVING, TEXAS
We stayed here with my mom's Uncle Ben and Aunt Teresa.

HOUSTON, TEXAS
I had to impress Béla and Márta Károlyi here to make it onto the US Olympic team. Then I went through grueling training at their gymnastics ranch to prepare for the Olympics.

HARTFORD, CONNECTICUT

After a competition here, my mom realized that I was improving so much in gymnastics that I needed a new coach. Hello, Liang Chow!

NEW YORK CITY

What haven't I done here?! From media appearances to competitions, I'll be back again soon, I'm sure!

VIRGINIA BEACH, VIRGINIA

Home sweet home. My grandmother, Carolyn Ford (who I call Miss Carolyn), lives here too!

International Locations

LONDON, ENGLAND

The biggest event of my life! 2012 Summer Olympics

TOKYO, JAPAN

Competing in Japan felt worlds away from Iowa or Virginia. I loved the gardens and the smell of miso soup in the streets.

JESOLO, ITALY

Gymnastics in Italy, amoré! (I competed here for the 2011 City of Jesolo Trophy.)

GUADALAJARA, MEXICO

I won my first international gold medal on uneven bars here at the 2010 Pan American Championships.

LET YOUR LIGHT SHINE BEFORE OTHERS, THAT THEY MAY SEE YOUR GOOD DEEDS AND GLORIFY YOUR FATHER IN HEAVEN.

—MATTHEW 5:16

Falling Back, Stepping Forward

As a competitive gymnast, I learned one lesson early: There's a thin line between winning and losing. Grabbing the gold often comes down to tiny point deductions. So if you want to be in first place—and that's always my goal!—you have to do your best and be as precise as you can with every single move you make on an apparatus. Just about every time I prepare for a competition, I ask God to focus my mind and strengthen my body so that I can perform at the highest level.

Here's the truth: No matter how careful I am or how hard I've trained, mistakes happen. During the 2012 Visa Championships in St. Louis, Missouri, I fell off the balance beam. A full point deduction! I was pretty disappointed. But I stayed focused on performing as well as I could on all the other apparatuses. It worked: Even after the fall, my overall score was only .2 less than the top one, so I won silver and earned a spot on the women's national team. Would I have jumped for joy if I'd won gold? Absolutely.

After so many years of competing, I've learned that your true courage often comes through when you're behind. For me, losing is motivation to keep reaching for my dream. Sometimes after a fall, I stand up a little taller and try a little harder the next time around. And once I do reach that top spot, let me tell you: There's no feeling like it!

That's why when I waved from the top of that Olympic podium—twice!—I thought not just of the many successes on the way to that goal; I also thought about the many missteps that had made me so much stronger.

Ups and Downs

I've definitely had my highs and lows in competition. Sometimes I've won first place. Other times I haven't even come close to earning a medal. Getting deductions or losing makes me work harder though. And working harder makes me better. Sometimes my competition has been more about contributing to my team than achieving my own goal. As discouraging as it is to fall, crash, or fail, I have to remember that it's all part of my path to success.

Losses

2012 OLYMPICS
didn't even come close to a medal on the uneven bars or balance beam

2012 VISA CHAMPIONSHIPS
fell off the beam twice

2010 PAN AMERICAN CHAMPIONSHIPS
fell twice on the beam, which ruled me out for the all-around

2010 COVERGIRL CLASSIC
placed only ninth in the all-around competition

2009 JUNIOR OLYMPIC NATIONAL CHAMPIONSHIP
crashed during my floor routine and came in fifth on the balance beam (due to my wrist fracture, I wasn't able to train consistently)

"YOU'RE GOING TO DO WHAT YOU'VE ALWAYS DONE—TRUST GOD TO CARRY YOU THROUGH IT," MOM TELLS ME. "YOU'VE GOT TO KEEP FIGHTING, BRIE."

Wins

2012 LONDON OLYMPICS
You already know what
happened, LOL!

2012 U.S. OLYMPIC TRIALS
first place in the
all-around competition

**2012 VISA CHAMPIONSHIPS
AND SECRET U.S. CLASSIC**
first place on uneven
bars at both events

**2010 PAN AMERICAN
CHAMPIONSHIPS**
my first international
gold medal on the
uneven bars

Team Wins

2012 OLYMPIC GAMES,
first place

**2012 KELLOGG'S PACIFIC
RIM CHAMPIONSHIPS**
first place

**2011 WORLD
CHAMPIONSHIPS**
first place

**2011 CITY
OF JESOLO TROPHY**
first place

**2010 PAN AMERICAN
CHAMPIONSHIPS**
first place

Rock Star Moment

I've had so many amazing moments since the Olympics, but one really stands out—the MTV Video Music Awards, otherwise known as the VMAs. On September 6, 2012, the Fierce Five (we've become like sisters) got all decked out so we'd be ready to walk the red carpet. I chose a gold-and-black sequined dress with black heel booties and the most adorable dangly earrings that worked perfectly with my long, loose hair. After I got my make-up done (someone was even polishing my fingers and toes!), the other girls and I climbed into a town car with tinted windows. When we finally stepped out of the car, the big crowd started chanting "U-S-A! U-S-A! U-S-A!" Once we were on the red car-pet, I got chills because of all the stars I spotted. We walked onto the red carpet behind Miley Cyrus. Later, we saw Katy Perry ("Gabby, I love you!" she yelled out), Rihanna, Taylor Swift . . .

I even got to perform on stage with the incredible Alicia Keys. I raced backstage to do the fastest clothing change of my life: I traded my dress for some black leather leggings and a flowing black top. I was so excited when Nicki Minaj rapped my name in her part of the song. As Alicia performed her hit song "Girl on Fire," I did handsprings across the stage. That's around the time my shirt flew up! No one saw anything, except for a little bit of my bra strap—but it certainly gave me a little scare, LOL. The whole night was one that I'll never (ever!) forget.

FOR GOD HATH NOT GIVEN US THE SPIRIT OF FEAR: BUT OF POWER, AND OF LOVE, AND OF A SOUND MIND.

2 TIMOTHY 1:7 (KJV)

#spotlight

Most of the time, it's fun to be famous—even if it does feel a little strange. Almost immediately after the London Olympics, celebs like Beyoncé and Oprah Winfrey actually sent me tweets! Who thought that they'd ever know my *name*?

For most of my life, I've been focused on a single goal: making it to the Olympics. That alone was exciting enough. So I wasn't exactly prepared for how it would feel to make history. As I stood on the podium to receive my gold medals, camera flashes lit up the stadium. How did I feel? Like a rock star. Seriously.

Since then, life has changed. First of all, I've developed some major muscle in my right arm because I've signed so many autographs! And here's the part I'm still getting used to: People I've never met recognize me. "Hey, Gabby!" they call out in the airport or a hotel lobby. "Good job!"

I enjoy meeting all the folks who come up to me, especially kids and teens. I want them to know that I'm exactly like they are—someone who had a dream. Not every person can get to the Olympics, but anyone can work hard toward a goal. So in a way, when I'm meeting other people, it's like meeting myself.

There is another side to fame: giving up some privacy. As much as I love posing for photos and chatting with new people, sometimes I just want to fly home to chill with my fam. When life on the road gets really busy (believe me, my feet have hardly touched the ground since London!), that's exactly what I do. But after a day or two, I'm ready for more—more camera flashes, more "Hi, Gabby!", more high-fives from people who see what's possible for themselves after they've seen what God made possible for me.

Gabrielle Douglas

@gabrielledoug

Wow! I have the most AMAZING FANS EVA! I have read a lot of great stories!

When I got back all I can say is....wow!!! #fanmail Thanks to all the support n love really means a lot!!!

don't feel like a celebrity. I still feel like a normal teen who got the extraordinary chance to see her dreams come true. But it's like I became an overnight celebrity. It's kind of weird but amazing to know that friends and fans come behind me with support. It's been fun to inspire everyone. I'm enjoying the attention and the chance to meet so many famous and inspiring people.

#fanmail

I t's my personality to smile and give out autographs. Once I gave out 480 autographs in forty-five minutes. Wow! I try to put myself in their shoes and enjoy it because it's gonna go by so fast. People won't want my autograph forever.

 Like **FACEBOOK LIKES:**

730,000+

 TWITTER FOLLOWERS: **750,000+**

I'm following 502 people on Twitter myself!

 INSTAGRAM FOLLOWERS: **444,000+**

One time, I asked my Twitter followers to send me their favorite jokes. Fun! Here's one that cracked me up.

 @collinFrye
@gabrielledoug 7. *How do celebrities stay cool? They have many fans! hahah this is you*

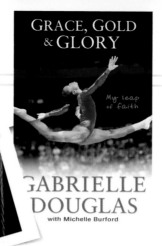

GRACE, GOLD & GLORY

My leap of faith

GABRIELLE DOUGLAS

with Michelle Burford

The Frenzy

My life after the Olympics put me in the center of the news. I can't believe how many interviews I've done. I traveled here and there to be in magazines, on TV shows, at award shows, and meet thousands of people. I even got to tell my story in my own book: *Grace, Gold & Glory.* Who knew that winning an Olympic medal would allow me to meet so many famous people like President and Mrs. Obama, Julia Roberts, Randy Jackson, and Anne Hathaway? How many sixteen-year-olds get that chance?

Back on Stage

The cast of my favorite TV show, *The Vampire Diaries*, filmed a special congratulations message for me. Damon (played by Ian Somerhalder) even blew me a kiss. They sent the video to me in London. Then I got an invitation to visit the set of the show and make a guest appearance in episode seven for the fall 2012 season. Mom and my sister Joy (also a fan!) were with me, so that made the whole day even more special. It was one of the best experiences of my life.

Nina Dobrev
@ninadobrev:

@gabrielledoug is coming to The Vampire Diaries set tomorrow! Cant wait to meet and work with you girl! Dont forget to bring your bling! :P

The Vampire Diaries
@vampirediaries:

@gabrielledoug @julie We can't wait to see you in #TVD episode 4.07, girl! Counting down the days! :-)

LET ALL THAT I AM PRAISE THE LORD; MAY I NEVER FORGET THE GOOD THINGS HE DOES FOR ME.

PSALM 103:2 (NLT)

What's Ahead

I'd love to go to college one day. I'd like to study acting and take some business classes. For now, I'm still finishing up my high-school diploma and focusing on my gymnastics training (Rio 2016, here I come!). Here's what I do know: I've definitely been bitten by the acting bug. So after high school and gymnastics, maybe acting is in my future. When I dream about what it might be like to act, I imagine playing all kinds of roles—from the nice girl to the diva.

But before thinking about college, I have to finish high school and get my driver's license, which is coming soon. When I lived in West Des Moines, Iowa, with my host family, Missy and Travis Parton, Travis began teaching me how to drive in his truck. The whole time, I'm like, "I'm gonna hit a deer!" He kept trying to calm me down, but seeing a deer kinda freaked me out. At least I got a little experience behind the wheel, with more to come.

Whether I choose a university, or something totally different (isn't it hard to know what you'll do tomorrow, not to mention years from now?), one thing is sure: With the Lord's help, I figured out my purpose—and I know he'll help me figure out my future.

GRACE, GOLD & GLORY

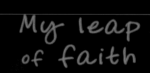

My leap of faith

GABRIELLE DOUGLAS

with Michelle Burford

Want to know more about what my life was like before the two gold medals? Pick up a copy of *Grace, Gold, & Glory: My Leap of Faith*. From my birth to the 2012 London games, I've faced lots of challenges and joys, and can't wait to share my story with you!